⪡ CHILDREN OF THE MAYA

⪅ CHILDREN

A Guatemalan Indian Odyssey

DODD, MEAD & COMPANY *New York*

OF THE MAYA ≈

Brent Ashabranner

Photographs by Paul Conklin

1 2 3 4 5 6 7 8 9 10

Library of Congress Cataloging-in-Publication Data

Ashabranner, Brent K., date
  Children of the Maya.

  Bibliography: p.
  Includes index.
  Summary: Examines the plight of Mayans who have fled
the violent political situation in Guatemala and
settled in a community in southern Florida.
  1. Kanjobal Indians—Social conditions—Juvenile
literature. 2. Indians of Central America—Guatemala—
Social conditions—Juvenile literature. 3. Mayas—
Social conditions—Juvenile literature. 4. Indiantown
(Fla.)—Social conditions—Juvenile literature.
5. Refugees, Political—Guatemala—Juvenile literature.
6. Refugees, Political—Florida—Juvenile literature.
[1. Mayas—Social conditions. 2. Indians of Central
America—Social conditions. 3. Guatemala—Politics
and government. 4. Indiantown (Fla.)—Social conditions.
5. Refugees] I. Conklin, Paul. II. Title.
F1465.2.K36A84 1986   975.9'31'00497   85–32537
ISBN 0-396-08786-8

This book is for the many people of Indiantown, Florida, who helped the Mayan Indians in their time of need.

≈ CONTENTS

Author's Note

GUATEMALAN Indian refugees now living in Indiantown, Florida, are the main subject of this book. They accepted me and my colleague, Paul Conklin, because we were introduced by some of the good people of Indiantown whom they know and trust. Those people are Neil Boothby, Sister Esperanza Jassa, Antonio Lazana, and Sister Carol Putnam, all of whom we thank very much. We also thank Francisco Pascual Aguirre, Jeronimo Camposeco, Sister Joan Gannon, Sebastian Torres, and Thelma Waters, all of Indiantown, who helped us in many ways. We are grateful to Duncan Earle, Professor of Anthropology, Dartmouth College, for use of his photographs taken in Guatemala.

For security reasons, I have changed the names of Guatemalan refugees and the villages from which they came. The names of other villages and towns where violence occurred are real.

Brent Ashabranner

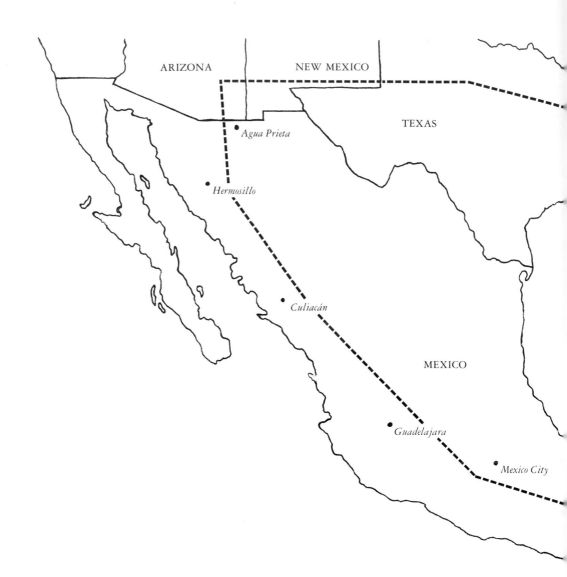

Mayan mother and children at Blue Camp.

≈ A SMALL TOWN IN FLORIDA

INDIANTOWN—so named because it was a campsite for Seminole Indians a hundred years ago—is not a place one would choose for a Florida vacation; but, as small rural towns go, it has its points. Its new intermediate school is well staffed and well equipped, and it has more churches than most places with a population of 3,500 are likely to have. Indiantown isn't big enough for a McDonald's or a Wendy's, but it does have an ice-cream parlor and a fast-food fried chicken drive-in. Two small supermarkets compete on the main street. Some nice homes on nice streets signal money in the community, and Big Mound Park has a good, well-lighted baseball field.

But Indiantown has another side. Some parts of town are jammed with run-down trailers and tiny cinder block houses where, from November to June, two or even three families live crowded together. In front of many of these places stand battered gas-guzzler cars and decrepit station wagons that look ready for the junkyard. Two big buildings in town, known as Yellow Camp and Blue Camp because of the color of their paint, are packed with single men and families who live in small one- and two-room units. Yellow Camp is known to Indiantowners as the "Roach Palace."

Yellow Camp, now occupied by many Mayan families. "Roach Palace" is no longer an appropriate nickname for the building. The owner has made major improvements for his tenants.

Mayan refugee.

Sister Esperanza Jassa, principal of Hope Rural School, helps Mayan student. The English meaning of "Esperanza" is "hope." As the students learn English, some of them have begun calling her Sister Hope.

as if their sandals were painted on their feet," she says, in a haunting metaphor.

Word went around Indiantown soon enough that these unusual newcomers were Mayan Indians from Guatemala, that the language most of them spoke was called Kanjobal, and that most came from an area of that country around a town named San Miguel Acatán. They all told stories of their villages in Guatemala being attacked by the Guatemalan army, of being harassed by guerrillas, of friends and relatives being killed.

But why Indiantown? What had led them four thousand miles to this small town in Florida? Sister Carol Putnam, a Sacred Heart nun who started Hope Rural School, mainly for migrant children, remembers when the Mayan Indians began to arrive in some numbers.

"It was the fall of 1982," she says. "I was talking with some of our schoolchildren about the Indians in Guatemala, and we decided to say a prayer for them. The very next week the first ones came to Indiantown in a migrant crew from another state. And they kept coming."

The migrant farmworker stream doubtless brought some Guatemalan Indians accidentally to Indiantown. Word surely went out from those already there to relatives in Guatemala and others who were refugees in Mexico. Beyond that, who can say what led them to this unlikely place? For whatever reasons, their numbers increased steadily until today more than five hundred Maya live there.

Paul and I first visited Indiantown in 1984 when we were gathering material for a book about migrant farmworkers. We returned a year later because we could not forget what we had seen there. We could

Mayan mother and child.

Mayan father and children.

not forget the faces of the Mayan men and women. We could not forget the way the people of Indiantown had helped these refugees whose need was so great. In the months that had passed, we had read dozens of reports and articles about the conflict in Guatemala that had forced the Mayan Indians to flee for their very lives. Now we wanted to hear the story from their own mouths, and most of all, we wanted to see the children again.

A year can make a great difference in the life of a child. The Mayan children were already on the road to regaining their health at the time of our first visit. Now they were the picture of health. They were riding bicycles, playing soccer in the parks and schoolyard, and scrambling for their turns on swings and jungle gym.

A year ago hardly any of the children would say a word to us, although some had learned a good deal of English. They weren't exactly chatterboxes now, but they would talk. I sat with Juana one day at Hope School while she ate her lunch. She told me that she still liked tortillas and beans best, which were about her only food in Guatemala, but that now she also liked fried fish and peanut butter and jelly sandwiches.

"Do you like pizza?" I asked.

"Yuck," she said.

A Mayan boy named Jose seemed to think that I was Popeye or at least that I looked like Popeye, and he apparently convinced one of his friends that I was that famous character. They both called me Popeye throughout my visit. Now, I don't think I look a bit like Popeye, but it was fine with me if they thought so. We had something to talk about.

"Is Popeye your favorite cartoon?" I asked Jose.

"No," he said, "Spiderman."

One day Jose was not in school, and I asked his teacher if she knew why. "His parents kept him out this morning," she said, "so that he can translate for them. They have business at the post office and electric company."

I learned that a good many parents have their children translate for them. Most of the adult Maya are learning some English but at a slower pace than their children.

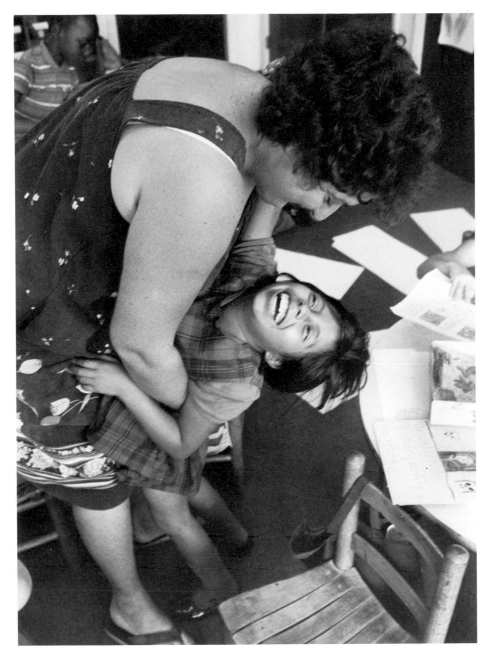

Juana, age ten, with her teacher, Mrs. Elizabeth Henriquez. Juana and her parents walked through Mexico; she arrived in Indiantown badly malnourished but is now the picture of health. "I like peanut butter and jelly, chicken, bananas, apples, and tortillas," says Juana.

Mayan children are quickly adjusting to life in Indiantown—riding bikes, playing video games, watching television.

During our days in Indiantown, I visited many Mayan families in their homes and listened to their stories. In the pages ahead I have told some of those stories and have given some background about the Mayan Indians and about the problems they have had in Guatemala. I have not attempted to tell the whole story of today's political turmoil in Guatemala and the rest of Central America. Other recent books have covered that subject, and some of them are listed in the bibliography. *Children of the Maya* is a book about people trying to survive in a world that has fallen apart.

≈ THE FURY

BETWEEN 1980 and 1984 the national army of Guatemala carried out a campaign of terror and dislocation against the Mayan Indians who live in the central and western highlands of that country. By its own count, the army destroyed 440 villages and damaged many others. Over thirty thousand Indians were killed. Another 150,000 fled to Mexico and settled in or near refugee camps close to the border; a much smaller number traveled the length of Mexico, mostly on foot, to reach the United States. At least a million more abandoned their villages and sought refuge in the forests and cities of Guatemala.

The Guatemalan government ordered or agreed to the army's campaign against the Mayan Indians because the mountainous areas where they live were becoming a stronghold of guerrilla rebels. The forests and rugged terrain of those parts of the country offer good hiding places for the guerrillas, and they can approach the Indian villagers for recruits and for food and money. A number of Indians have joined the guerrillas.

Mayan houses in Guatemala.

Duncan Earle

General Efraín Ríos Montt (center) with Guatemalan army staff members. Violence against the Mayan Indians reached its height after Montt became Guatemala's president in a coup d'etat in March, 1982.

Like Nicaragua and El Salvador, Guatemala for years has contended with an armed rebel movement that wants to bring about political changes and social reforms. Compared to those other Central American countries, however, the number of guerrilla rebels in Guatemala has been small, by most estimates never numbering more than six thousand, and perhaps no more than four thousand.

The army's fury, nevertheless, has descended on the Mayan people as a whole. Through massacres, destruction of villages, and burning of crops, the army's clear purpose has been to terrorize the Indians, to make them afraid to support the guerrillas in any way.

The army's ultimate objective, in fact, has been to disrupt the Indian villagers' lives so totally that they would be unable to give the rebels any help even if they wanted to.

This violence against its own people by the Guatemalan army has gone largely unnoticed in the United States because of our preoccupation with El Salvador and Nicaragua, but it has been well documented. Courageous voices even in Guatemala have been raised against what is happening. In May, 1982, the Guatemala Bishops' Conference issued a statement which described the army's program of fear and death against the country's Indians as genocide—the deliberate destruction of a racial or cultural group. That same month, *El Grafico,* Guatemala's largest and most prestigious newspaper, printed an editorial about the army's terror campaign which contained this statement:

> To anyone who has any sympathy with his fellow man, the kind of genocidal annihilation that is taking place in the Indian zones of the country is truly horrifying. Anyone who has children or grandchildren or a brother or a mother has to be in disagreement, has to energetically condemn these merciless massacres.

Shortly after that editorial, Rios Montt, then president of Guatemala, imposed strict censorship on the country's press.

In September, 1984, a report of the Guatemala Supreme Court estimated that 100,000 children had lost as least one parent in the massacres and that 20 percent of those had lost both parents. Later estimates raised the number of children who had lost one or both parents to between 150,000 and 200,000.

"Guatemala is now a nation of orphans," a Guatemalan journalist wrote, in an act of considerable personal courage.

A number of international organizations have documented the

Guatemalan government's war against its Indian population. Some of those issuing reports are the Organization of American States, the United Nations Commission on Human Rights, and Amnesty International. The British Parliamentary Human Rights Group, which is made up of members of both houses of Parliament, issued a report entitled *Bitter and Cruel.* Two subcommittees of the U. S. Congress also have reported on human rights violations in Guatemala.

≈LAND OF THE ANCIENTS

T H E   M O S T beautiful country in the world: that is what many experienced travelers have called Guatemala. Certainly, it is one of the most beautiful. Tall mountain ranges sweep from border to border. Majestic volcanoes, their cones shrouded in clouds, sit at the edge of lovely lakes. Mountains, windswept plateaus, green valleys, dense lowland jungles, and Pacific beaches bring rich variety to this small country.

About 2000 B.C., in this land of mountains and jungles, a mysterious Indian people, the Maya, established their culture and developed a great civilization. Their empire stretched from what is now southern Mexico through much of Central America. The ancient Maya are a mystery because we have been able to learn very little about the origins of this magnificent culture and are equally baffled as to why it disappeared about A.D. 900.

For many years, through excavations and by clearing away jungle growth, archaeologists and anthropologists have been learning more about the accomplishments of these remarkable people. Their sacred

Mayan ruins.

cities, with temples and pyramids rising to fifteen stories, rivaled those of Egypt in their splendor. The Maya became astronomers and built great stone observatories. They charted the skies, tracking the course of the planet Venus with an accuracy almost matching that of modern scientists who use radar and telescopes. Astronomers today calculate the solar year as being 365.2420 days. The Maya calculated it at 365.2422—a difference of but a few seconds!

The Maya developed a complex social, political, and legal system. They created a written hieroglyphic language and were one of only three civilizations in history to independently develop the concept of the number zero. Their achievements in engineering, architecture, law, and social organization matched those of the classical Greek civilization. Their artists produced powerful stone sculpture and elegant ceramics, masks, and jewelry.

One thing is clearly known about the ancient Mayan civilization: it had its beginnings in a simple food grain—corn. The discovery of corn by the Maya perhaps as much as four thousand years ago changed them from a nomadic hunting and plant-gathering people. With the domestication of corn, they did not have to be constantly on the move and could supply their food needs with much less effort. Out of this increased leisure and the ability to live in one place came, over centuries, the great cities and achievements in science and art. The Maya also developed a complex religion, and it is no surprise that their most important and most revered god was Yum Kax, the god of corn.

And then all was gone. The cities, temples, and observatories were abandoned, the scientific knowledge lost except for a few sacred books that survived. Whether because of war, internal strife, drought, disease epidemics, or all of those things, the Mayan civilization crumbled centuries before the Spanish conquest, which began in 1519.

Dancers in Mayan Conquest Dance in Guatemala. Traditions have been carried through the centuries.

There would seem to be little connection between the 3.5 million Indians of Guatemala today and the Maya of ancient times. In fact, the connection is direct and unbroken. Even in the golden centuries of the Mayan civilization, the vast majority of people were farmers who lived in villages and worked hard every day growing corn and other crops. The women of the village sometimes worked in the fields but spent most of their time grinding corn, cooking, weaving cloth, and making pots.

These people lived simply, but religion, as they learned it from the Mayan priests, was a fundamental part of their lives. Although they understood little of what was happening in the cities, their labor provided wealth on which kings built an empire.

The daily life of most present-day Maya in Guatemala is remarkably similar to that of their rural ancestors. Corn is still at the heart of their existence; everything else is secondary to its cultivation. Even the planting stick, to make a hole for the seed corn, that most farmers use is the same as their earliest forefathers used. Women still grind corn on a volcanic stone called a *metate,* just as their ancestors did. They weave cloth and make pots with designs that reach back through the mists of time.

Although most now have Spanish names and have accepted Christianity, the Maya of today have not forgotten the ancient gods of their people. The Indian's life still depends on corn, and many say prayers and make offerings to the corn god and rain god to ensure the corn's proper growth. Most villages have a prayer maker who knows the right forms for these prayers and for others that should be said when a house is to be blessed or when one of the Year Bearers, gods who bring the new year, must be asked for good health and protection.

"The customs of the Ancient Ones have never been changed," a prayer maker once told Maud Oakes, an anthropologist who lived in a Mayan village in Guatemala. "If a man changes these customs, he dies. We do not play with the things of God."

In the *departamento* (state) of Huehuetenango in western Guatemala, the rugged Cuchumatanes Mountains soar to eleven thousand feet, and villages can be found as high as eight thousand feet. On the slopes of the Cuchumatanes, farmers raise corn, beans, wheat, and sheep. In the lower plains, where the *departamento* forms part of the border with Mexico, plantation owners grow coffee, sugarcane, and tropical fruit.

In Indiantown, Mayan refugees attend Mass at Holy Cross Church.

The rainy, cloud-covered highlands of Huehuetenango are Mayan country. The very name Huehuetenango means "Place of the Ancients." Over a quarter of a million Indians live here. They speak the Mam, Jacaltec, Kanjobal, and Chuj languages, but all are descended from the Ancient Ones.

During the summer of 1980, the *departamento* of Huehuetenango was drawn into the conflict between guerrillas and the national military that previously had been confined mainly to the central highlands and the plantation areas of the coastal lowlands. An

26

organization that calls itself the Guerrilla Army of the Poor began sending groups of its members into villages, usually at night. They would speak to the villagers about the evils of the government, distribute propaganda leaflets, and then leave. In some cases they demanded food and money.

The Guatemalan army is the best equipped and trained military force in Central America. It responded to the guerrilla challenge by increasing its troops in the departmental capital city, which is also named Huehuetenango. It brought in more trucks, helicopters, and other military equipment.

The fury was about to begin for the Indian people of the Cuchumatanes highlands.

Mayan farmer, going to the fields in Guatemala.

～JUAN SALAZAR

What else could I do?

JUAN SALAZAR was born in Tres Valles, a village of perhaps five hundred people not far from the large market town of San Miguel Acatán and a two-hour bus ride from the city of Huehuetenango, which everyone calls Huehue. Juan's father and grandfather and even his great-grandfather were born in Tres Valles. Juan remembers once asking his great-grandfather how long Tres Valles had been there.

"Why, always," his great-grandfather told him. "What a foolish question."

When he was nineteen, Juan married a Tres Valles girl who was seventeen. They both worked hard and in time owned about twenty acres of land on which they grew corn and wheat. They had a small flock of sheep and two horses. It was not a great deal, but it was enough to provide for them and their two sons and one daughter. They lived in a large one-room adobe house which they whitewashed every year after the rainy season, and one year ago they had replaced their thatched roof with one made of tiles.

Juan and his two sons worked in their fields and tended the sheep. His older son, Rafael, who was thirteen, was strong and a good worker, and Jose, who was but eight, was learning to be a good helper, especially with the sheep. The family ate four pounds of corn every day, and Mrs. Salazar seemed always to be grinding corn and making tortillas. But she also washed clothes at the *pila,* the village fountain, and she wove bright cotton cloth on a loom that had belonged to her mother and grandmother. Their seven-year-old daughter, Teresa, was learning to do all of those things. Although tortillas and beans were their daily diet, on Sundays Mrs. Salazar made a stew of mutton and, at very special times, of beef, with peppers and potatoes.

Theirs was a hard life but good, and then everything changed. This is the way Juan Salazar remembers it:

I HAD HEARD about guerrillas coming to villages in Huehuetenango, but I did not know if it was true. I thought perhaps that people were just making up stories as they sometimes like to do. But then one night the guerrillas came to Tres Valles. I do not remember exactly when, but it was sometime in the spring of 1981. There were eight or ten of them, some Indians, some *ladinos*—people of mixed Spanish and Indian descent. They all had guns. I do not know about guns, but they looked new and powerful. The guerrillas did not stay long that first time, but they said they would come back.

They did come back, many times and even more of them. They came to our house and to every house in Tres Valles, and they said that every family must send at least one member to a meeting to listen to the guerrilla leader. I did not want to go, but they had guns and they had beaten a man in public that night because he refused to go.

30

I told them I would go for my family, but they said Rafael must come too because he would soon be old enough to fight. They said they had boys who were not much older than thirteen.

At the meeting the guerrilla leader said that the Indians must join all others in fighting government soldiers and making a new government and that someday we would be rich and have cars to drive. It sounded like crazy talk to me, but we were all afraid because they had guns and we had nothing but machetes, which we used in our fields and not for fighting. I do not know if anyone from Tres Valles joined them, but they came other times that spring and summer. They demanded food and sometimes money. I wondered why soldiers did not come from Huehue to keep the guerrillas away from our village, but no one came.

Up to that time in the summer of 1981 we had not even seen the army, but then one day we did. It was Sunday, July 19. You do not forget such a day. Our family was on the road to San Rafael to sell potatoes in the market there. Everyone likes market day. We see our friends from other villages and exchange news, and when we have sold what we have brought that day, there will be candy for the children. Even Rafael liked candy, though he pretended it was for the little ones.

We were only a short time on our journey when there was a great noise, and five big army trucks drove past us. I had to get everyone off the road in a hurry, as well as our horse carrying the potatoes, or we would have been smashed. When the trucks pulled ahead of us, they stopped, and one of the drivers asked me if this was the road to Coyá, which is a small village where Indians who speak the Migdeleño tongue live. I told him that it was.

Then one of the soldiers in the truck nearest to us shouted, "I think we should kill these people. They are probably guerrillas."

A market in the Indian highlands of Guatemala.

I could not believe what I had heard, and I thought he was joking. "I am a farmer from Tres Valles," I said. "We are on our way to sell potatoes in San Rafael."

An officer got out of a truck and said, "No. We don't want any gunshots now." And then he gave an order for the trucks to go on.

I did not want to go to San Rafael after that, and we turned back toward Tres Valles, but on the way we stopped on a high hill and looked toward Coyá, which was just a few kilometers away. While we watched, two helicopters flew over Coyá and hovered there. We could hear explosions and gunfire. Then an airplane came from the direction of Huehue and dropped bombs on Coyá. It seemed to me that the explosions and the gunfire went on for a long time, but I do not know how long it was. I was troubled and afraid, and I took my family home.

That night a few people from Coyá came to Tres Valles. Most of them had been shot or hacked with machetes. Even those who were not wounded seemed more dead than alive. They said that soldiers from the trucks had surrounded Coyá and kept anyone from escaping while the plane dropped bombs, and machine guns were fired from the helicopters. After that the soldiers went to every house, shooting, stabbing, and clubbing everyone they could find. They spared no one, not even children, women, or the oldest people in the village.

"We cannot go back," said one woman. "It is a place of dead people."

Why did the army do such a thing? Coyá is no different from any other village in Huehuetenango. Some people said that they did it so that every Indian in every village would be afraid to help the guerrillas. But how could such a thing be?

After that, soldiers did start to come to Tres Valles. They would warn us not to help guerrillas, and they would question people about their neighbors. One day they took away three men from Tres Valles, and we never saw them again. Their families could never learn anything about them. But at night, when the soldiers were gone, the guerrillas would come back and threaten us if we did not give them food. They killed one man who told them he did not have enough food for his own family.

Our daughter, Teresa, began to have terrible nightmares about me being taken away by the army and not coming back. Our son Jose would cry at the sound of any airplane or helicopter. Because he was thirteen and big, Rafael did not cry and he tried not to show his fear, but he was afraid, and he had every reason to be. At any time the guerrillas might force him to join them, and at any time the army might kill him to keep him from joining the guerrillas. Does that sound insane? But it was true that the army was now beginning to murder men and older boys just because they might become guerrillas.

In the town of San Mateo Ixtatán, soldiers broke into houses at night and killed thirty-six people. That was even before Coyá. I had heard about it but did not believe it. Now I did. In the village of Suntelaj, which is very near Tres Valles, soldiers rounded up fifteen people and killed them with grenades. My wife and I knew some of the widows.

Over a year went by from the time that the army destroyed Coyá. Rafael was fourteen now and in more danger every day. My wife wanted me to take our two sons and go to Mexico. Others from our village had already done that. But how could I? How could I leave my wife and daughter? How could I leave my parents and the holy ground of my ancestors? How could I leave the home and land I had worked a lifetime for? What would I do in Mexico or anywhere else on earth except Tres Valles?

And yet I knew that if I loved my sons I had to take them away. I said to my wife that we should all leave together, but she said no, that the three of us alone would have a better chance. And so one night when it was very dark we left, saying good-bye to no one, and walked until we crossed the border into Mexico.

What else could I do?

After several months in a refugee camp near the Mexican border, Juan Salazar and his two sons walked the length of Mexico to the Arizona border and crossed into the United States. Working as mi-

Mayan man in Indiantown.

grant farm laborers, they made their way to Indiantown, Florida, where Mr. Salazar knew that he had a cousin who also had fled from Guatemala. In Indiantown, Mr. Salazar made contact with his wife and learned that life was becoming very dangerous in Tres Valles for women without their husbands.

Calling upon church friends in the city of Huehuetenango, Mr. Salazar arranged for the escape of his wife and daughter from Guatemala. Their journey through Mexico was long and frightening, but today the Salazar family is living together in Indiantown.

≈LUIS GARCIA

A picture of my family

LUIS GARCIA is sixteen. He was born in the village of Rincón, which is not far from Tres Valles and Suntelaj, and lived there all his life with his father, mother, and two younger brothers and two younger sisters. His father was a farmer, like almost every other man in Rincón, and Luis helped him on the small piece of land where they grew corn and beans.

At one time Rincón had a primary school, which is now closed because no teacher will stay there since the terror began. But while it was there, Luis attended and learned to read and write. Although they were poor, Mr. and Mrs. Garcia wanted their children to get as much schooling as possible. They were a close and loving family, and Luis's story of what happened, as he tells it here, is but one example of similar tragedy that has come to thousands of Indian families in Guatemala.

DO YOU KNOW the word *orejas?* It means ears, but when we say it in our villages in Guatemala now, it is one of the worst words in the world. It means people who listen and then tell the soldiers who come to the villages what they have heard or think they have heard or seen. They are people who have always lived in the village, but they have become spies for the army. Or maybe they make up things to tell the soldiers so that the soldiers will pay them or leave them alone.

I do not know how many *orejas* were in our village of Rincón. There is no way for any village to know. But if there is only one, or even none, our villages are not the same as they once were. Before the guerrillas and the army came, before there were *orejas,* the people of Rincón would walk the streets in the evening after the day's work was done. They would talk to neighbors and friends and gather at the *pila* or in front of the church and tell what news they had heard or just gossip. They were not afraid and they were happy.

Now no one goes out at night. The streets are empty, and no one gathers at the *pila* or in front of the church. No one talks to his neighbors, and everyone locks his doors. That is what Rincón is like now and what all villages in Huehuetenango are like.

In Rincón there were *orejas,* or at least one, and my father was killed because of that. Guerrillas came to our village as much as twice a month, and they often came to our house. Maybe it was because I was fifteen then and old enough to join them. I do not know. But my father always talked to them and said I was needed at home to help support the big family. Sometimes we had to give them food and sometimes a little money, though my father had almost none to give. They threatened to kill us if he did not.

Someone told the army that my father was helping the guerrillas, and one night four soldiers came to our house. When they banged on the door, my father knew what it was, and he climbed out the back window and ran. The soldiers said that they knew my father was helping guerrillas and that maybe he was with them now. They said they would find him, and they left.

Young Mayan boys at Hope Rural School in Indiantown. In some Guatemalan villages, schools have been closed because of the terror.

My father walked to San Miguel Acatán, and a friend hid him in his house. But the soldiers found him. They beat him and then shot him and cut off his head. They killed his friend, too, and threw them both in a ditch.

The next day we found my father and carried him home. We washed him and put him in a coffin. I remember that his head did not fit very well with his body. It is something I wish I could forget, but I can't.

After that the guerrillas came to our house again, and this time they pointed a gun at me and stuck a knife to my throat and said they would kill me if I didn't join them. I said I would but that they would have to give me a week to get ready. I knew I would not join them, though I didn't know what I would do.

But my mother said that I must leave Rincón and go to Mexico. I told her I did not want to leave, but she said that if I didn't either the guerrillas or the army would kill me. I asked her how she and my brothers and sisters could live if there was no one to plant corn and harvest the crops. She said she would get her father and my father's brother to help.

So I walked to Mexico. I was fifteen and afraid to go by myself, but I had to go. I walked at night and hid in the forests in the daytime. Near the border is a free-fire zone where soldiers will shoot on sight anyone they see. But I crossed the border into Mexico at night, and I did not see any soldier.

Because I had been to school, I could speak and read some Spanish, and that helped. I did not go to a refugee camp because I was afraid they would send me back to Guatemala. I went to the town of Motozinitia, and after a while I got a job working on houses. I made enough money to buy food and I lived in a little room in the house of the man I worked for.

I had never been by myself before, and there was nothing in the world I wanted as much as to be back in Rincón. Sometimes I would meet someone who had come from someplace near San Miguel Acatán, and I would ask if it was safe to go back there. They always told me I should not even think about going back.

But I could not help thinking about it. It was hot in Mexico, and I thought about the cool mountains at home. I thought about how my father used to take us to the fiesta in San Rafael, how we would drink *frescas* and eat candy and fly kites. I thought about *pan dulce,* the sweet cornbread my mother made for special times, and I could almost taste it.

But mostly I thought about my mother and my brothers and sisters, and I wondered what was happening to them. The wife of the man I worked for gave me a magazine, and when I was looking through it one night, I saw a picture of a woman with four children, two boys and two girls. I tore the picture out of the magazine and pinned it on the wall of my room. I pretended it was a picture of my family, of my mother and sisters and brothers.

One morning I woke up and knew that I could not stay in Mexico by myself any longer. I knew there was a place in the United States called Indiantown, in a place called Florida, where an uncle and aunt of mine had gone when they escaped from Guatemala with their children. I did not know if they were still there, but since I could not go back to my home, I decided to go to Indiantown and try to find them.

When I had saved enough money to buy a bus ticket to the United States border, I left Motozinitia. Before I left, I took down the picture from the wall and took it with me.

Luis Garcia reached Indiantown and found his uncle and aunt. He is now living with them and his cousins and working as a farm laborer. His mother and brothers and sisters are still in Guatemala.

41

One of the few Mayan intermediate school students in Indiantown. He writes stories about his village on a computer.

⇌ ANTONIO GUERRA

We walked a long time

ONE OF THE most hated and feared actions of the Guatemalan army is the conscription of Indian youth into the military service. In the slang of the country it is called *el cupo,* "the grab." There is nothing new about military conscription in Guatemala. For years the army has gone into rural villages and simply seized young men. Those who could not immediately prove they were under eighteen, in school, or married and supporting children were taken away and conscripted into the army for two years of service.

With the increase of guerrilla activity in the Indian areas of the country, the army greatly accelerated its conscription, concentrating on young Indian men. The chief tactic was to descend without warning on a village, seal off all roads, and begin a search through the streets and even into houses. The army would seize all young men it could find who looked as if they might be between eighteen and twenty-one years old. But in many cases Indian youths of sixteen and seventeen and sometimes even fifteen were picked up. If they could not prove their age—and in most cases they could not—they were put in trucks and hauled off to the nearest army installation for "recruitment." Sometimes parents were close by and could produce proof of their son's age, but that happened only for the lucky few.

Another favorite trick of the army conscriptors was to swoop down on a town market or fiesta and haul away any young men who could not escape. The fear of "the grab" without doubt drove some young Indian men into joining guerrilla bands.

A different but equally hated practice of the army was the forming of civil guard units in every village and town in the Indian highlands. These units were made up of men as old as seventy and boys as young as thirteen. They were supposed to take turns being on duty day and night, and since a village would number only a few hundred people, this service in the civil guard or citizens' militia, as it was sometimes called, took time away from work in the fields that caused serious hardships.

The civil guard units were supposed to keep guerrillas from coming into the villages, but they were given no serious training and no means of confronting the guerrillas. They had sticks and machetes which they supplied themselves, hardly a match for the guns the guerrillas carried. Perhaps the greatest evil of the civil guard was that the army sometimes made guard members join in acts of terrorism against other villagers. Enrollment in the civil guard was supposed to be voluntary. In practice, any person who refused to join risked being beaten or killed as a guerrilla sympathizer.

But in most cases it was the brutal, senseless killing of civilians by the army, their destruction of villages and burning of crops that convinced thousands of Indian peasant farmers in Guatemala that their only hope was to flee from the country. Antonio Guerra, a man who wanted very much to stay, tells why he led his family on a long and painful journey to escape the army's cruelty.

N O, I W A S not afraid of "the grab." Some of my good friends had sons taken away, one of them on his sixteenth birthday. But I had only two daughters, so that was one worry I did not have. I have always wanted a son, but I thanked God that I did not have one who might have been taken by "the grab" or by the guerrillas.

Yes, I was in the civil guard, twice a week, sometimes all day, sometimes all night. To have said no to the army when they asked you to join would have been very dangerous. Being in the civil guard would have been dangerous, too, if we had tried to stop the guerrillas from entering our village. Could you say to a man carrying a rifle or a pistol, "Don't come in this place or I will hit you with my stick?" We would call to the people that the guerrillas were coming, but that was all we could do.

It was not "the grab" or the civil guard or the guerrillas that made me decide to leave my country. It was the army, what they did to my village. My family and I lived in a village not far from Barillas and San Mateo Ixtatán. My wife and I were born in Tres Valles and married there. I spent much time picking coffee on the large plantations on the coast so that we could save money to buy a piece of land, and finally we did save enough.

We moved to the village near Barillas because the land is more fertile there. We bought fifteen acres of uncultivated land. We cleared it and fertilized it, and in time our crops were good ones. We grew corn and wheat and cardamom, which is good to sell for cash. Sometimes I still went to the coast to pick coffee when we needed more money to improve our land.

Both of our daughters were born in our new home. Estela was thirteen and Angelica was but three at the time we are talking about. Not a big family but we loved them very much and wanted to make a good home for them. Our house was not very big, but it was big

Mayan refugee sisters, Indiantown, a long way from home.

enough for us. Our village was where we wanted to live all our lives and where we wanted our daughters to grow up and marry.

There are many villages in the area around Barillas and San Mateo Ixtatán. Late in 1981 the guerrillas started coming into the villages. They came to ours many times and to our house asking for food and money. I was worried because I knew what the army had done at Coyá and Suntelaj and other places around San Miguel Acatán. I knew, too, about the people who had been killed one night in San Mateo Ixtatán, just a few months before, in June.

But for the last part of 1981 and the first six months of 1982 we had no problem with the military. Sometimes we saw soldiers in trucks and sometimes they stopped in our village, but there was no trouble. And then came July. The army began to attack villages near ours—Aguacate, Petanac, Yalanbojoch, and others. In some a few people were killed, in others, many. Houses were burned, crops were burned, cattle were driven away. I knew those places and saw people from them, so I knew it was true. I thought about leaving and taking my wife and daughters to Mexico as I knew many others had done. But I still could not believe that the army would attack my village. I did not want to believe it. And so I stayed.

One day, late in July, they came. I was at home that day, and I heard guns shooting and people shouting and screaming. I opened the door and saw people running and soldiers in camouflage uniforms shooting people. Then I heard another sound and two helicopters came over our village and bullets came down from them, machine gun bullets, I think. I smelled smoke and saw that some houses at the edge of the village were burning.

I shut the door and did not know what to do. If we tried to run away, they would shoot at us. If we stayed in the house, we might be burned. What a terrible choice. Finally, my wife and I hid Estela and Angelica in a corner beneath a pile of blankets, and we waited and listened to the terrible sounds outside.

And then the soldiers and the helicopters went away, and there was only the sound of people crying and calling the names of their children. Many people were killed and wounded, women and children as well as men. The soldiers did not care as long as they killed. Some houses were burned. Why ours was spared only God knows. But it made no difference. I knew that I must take my wife and children away. The army might come back, as it had done in other villages.

Before we left, we all took a bath in our *temascal*. A *temascal* is a sweat house, a small building that stands beside an Indian's house in Guatemala. Inside is an oven or stove made of small stones. We make a fire with special wood. The room gets very hot and we cleanse ourselves. The Ancient Ones also had *temascals.* Our way of bathing has never changed. I did not know if we would ever use our *temascal* again, but I wanted us to use it once more.

After two months in a refugee settlement in Chiapas, Mexico, Mr. and Mrs. Guerra saw that their daughters' health, both physical and mental, was deteriorating. They saw no hope of their food and shelter improving, so they decided to try to find someplace else to live in Mexico. They went to Mexico City but soon left because of the ever-present immigration police. Mr. Guerra tried to find work in Guadalajara, Culiacán, and Hermosillo, moving always northward through Mexico with his family, but, except for occasional day labor, he found nothing. At that point he determined to try to take his family to the United States. Mr. Guerra tells about their journey.

I KNEW nothing about the United States, but I knew that if we stayed in Mexico we would starve or be caught by the immigration police and sent back to the refugee camps or to Guatemala. Any of those things meant death for my family. So in Hermosillo we sold a gold necklace that my wife's mother had given to her when we were married. Selling it was a sad moment for us, but what else was there to do? I know we did not get as much money for it as we should have, but it was enough to get us close to the border where Mexico and Arizona meet. A man in Hermosillo told me that the border near a Mexican town named Agua Prieta was a good place to try to cross.

When we reached a town near Agua Prieta, I bought two plastic bottles and we filled them with water, and we filled a large plastic box with tortillas. Then we started across the desert. We had no

Mayan family with their home in the background. Baby has been born since they arrived in Indiantown.

coyote—that is what men who guide illegal border crossers are called —to take us. They charge much money, and we did not have it.

I carried Angelica. My wife carried the tortillas, and Estela carried the water bottles. I was frightened, perhaps as frightened as when the soldiers attacked our village, but it was different. Then the fear was sudden. Now it was with me every hour that we walked. We walked at night and hid in the daytime. It was very cold at night and very hot during the day. I thought, what if we lose our way? What if we run out of water and food? There were no houses, no people, just sand and rocks and bushes. Sometimes I almost hoped that a border patrol helicopter would find us, but we saw nothing and no one.

I do not remember how many nights we walked. Perhaps four, perhaps five. I know we walked a long time. Estela's feet became very sore, and during the day my wife would rub them. The tortillas kept us from hunger, but we were always thirsty. We drank but twice a day and then only a little. When our first water bottle was empty, my fear grew larger.

I do not know when we crossed the border, but one night we came to a road and followed it. When I saw signs along the road that were in English, I knew that we were in the United States. At that time I had no idea of going to Florida. I had never heard of Florida. I had no idea at all except to find work on a farm anywhere I could.

I know now that we were very lucky. We might have died in the desert. We might have been arrested by the border patrol or the highway police because we walked on the highway many times. And I know there are bad people we might have met, but we met good people. Sometimes we received rides and sometimes people bought us food. I can speak Spanish, and we met people I could talk to.

A Mexican family in a truck gave us a ride, and the man told me about Florida. He said he had worked there and it was a good place for a man to find work on farms. I am glad now that I did not know how far away Florida was from Arizona or perhaps we would never have tried to reach it. But we did reach it, and after we were there I heard about Indiantown. We went there, and it was good to be with our own people and to speak Kanjobal again.

The Guerras are still in Indiantown, and now they have a third member of their family, a son.

ᗞCESAR MORALES

We could not live under a tree any longer

THE FLIGHT into Mexico of Guatemalan Indians escaping the army's atrocities in 1982 and 1983 was sudden and massive. The Mexican government, caught totally unprepared, set up a refugee relief commission, COMAR, and turned to the United Nations High Commission on Refugees for help. The refugees needed everything: food, water, shelter, medical help.

In 1984 the UNHCR estimated that almost 50,000 refugees were living in ninety official camps near the Mexico-Guatemala border in the state of Chiapas. Other Guatemalans, estimated at between 70,000 and 100,000, lived in refugee settlements that received no help from COMAR or the UN High Commission.

Life was wretched for the refugees and continues to be. Almost all of them left their Guatemalan villages in panic with no money and only the clothes and personal belongings they wore and could carry in a bag or basket. Those in the refugee camps live in flimsy huts of bamboo or boards; water comes from a pump or a river; cooking is done outside the hut over an open fire; firewood is sometimes scarce;

Derrill Bazzy

Overview of refugee camp in Chiapas, Southern Mexico, where in 1982, thousands of Mayan Indians fled Guatemala to avoid the massacres by the army there. This camp is called las cascadas, *"the waterfall," and is one of many camps along the border. About two hundred people live here. They all fled Guatemala when the village next to theirs was massacred.*

sanitary conditions are terrible. Food supplies from the refugee relief agencies are never enough; hunger and malnutrition are everywhere. One of the worst problems is boredom; there is nothing to do all day but sit. A few of the men get jobs working on farms or plantations; they are the lucky ones.

For those who cannot get into the refugee camps or are afraid to go into them, life is worse. The Catholic Church in Mexico and some private organizations do everything they can to help, but few refugees outside the camps have any kind of houses to live in, and less than half receive any help with food or medical supplies. As with those in the refugee camps, a few fortunate men find work, but most refugees live on food that is given to them and on roots and leaves that they find in the surrounding jungles.

Health problems are severe for all the refugees, whether they live in COMAR camps or in makeshift settlements. Malaria, dengue fever, tuberculosis, parasite infections, diarrhea, gastrointestinal infections, respiratory conditions: Almost all of the refugees have one or more of these afflictions. But severe malnutrition in the children is the specter that haunts every camp and settlement.

As if it has not already damaged the lives of these people enough, the Guatemalan army has sent more than seventy raiding patrols across the border to attack the refugees in the camps and settlements. Despite protests by the Mexican government, these raids have continued, and some camps have even been bombed by Guatemalan aircraft. Many of the refugees in the camps are women and children whose husbands and fathers have been killed by the Guatemalan army. In one destitute settlement, workers from a relief organization counted fifty-two orphans.

Because of the raids and because Chiapas is such a poor part of the country, the Mexican government has started to relocate some

54

of the refugees much farther away from the border. But the refugees do not want to be moved. They want to stay as near as possible to the homes from which they have been driven. The only hope for them is that someday they will be able to return.

Cesar Morales, his wife, and three children were refugees in Mexico for almost a year. Leaving their village in Huehuetenango had been an agonizing decision for Mr. Morales. He had a good farm, which had been given to him by his father. He had worked hard, saved his money, and had recently bought another piece of land. Guerrillas came to the village often looking for help, as they did to all the villages in the area. Twice army patrols came into the Morales' village and murdered people they said were helping the guerrillas.

Even then the guerrillas did not stop coming, and they came several times to Mr. Morales's house because they knew he had more money than most of the people in the village. He knew it was only a matter of time before someone reported him to the army and his name would be put on a death list. His wife and children begged him to leave and take them away, too. When a large army squad raided another village very near them, killed twenty people, and burned all the crops, Mr. Morales knew that by staying longer he was only endangering all their lives.

Once night they left their house and walked for several nights until they crossed the border into Mexico. Mr. Morales tells what it was like after that.

T H E R E W E R E so many *naturales*—that is what we, the Indians, call ourselves. I couldn't believe it—from everywhere in Huehuetenango and from so many other *departamentos:* Quiché, Alta Verapaz, San Marcos, Baja Verapaz. They all told the same stories, the same things that had happened in my village, and things even worse. We stayed for three days in a small settlement of a dozen families, all of whom spoke our language, which is Kanjobal.

I learned all that I could, and I decided not to try to get into a refugee camp. There probably was no space anyway, but if we were in a camp, we might be relocated to another part of Mexico—to Campeche, where they were beginning to send refugees. Campeche is a long way away, and I wanted to stay near our home.

Going back was the only thing I could think about, and I wondered everyday if I had made a mistake in leaving our village. And then one day a woman came to the settlement where we were staying. She was from our village in Guatemala. She told us that the army had returned and killed most of the people. They had killed her husband and two sons. I asked her when the army had returned. It was the day after my family and I had left. Then I never wondered again if I had made a mistake, but still my thoughts were of going back.

There was no hope of getting work where we were, so we went on and joined a settlement near Comitán, a big settlement of perhaps two hundred people, mostly from Huehuetenango but from other places, too. We had a few *quetzals*—that is Guatemalan money—and a gold necklace and ring that we sold for pesos, so we had a little money, but it did not last long.

We lived under a big mango tree. I used some of the money to buy canvas and boards, and my wife and I made a *champa,* a small shelter where at least the children could sleep. We spent much of our time looking for food in the forest, and we found roots and sometimes fruit but never enough. At other times we would wait where the church workers brought food—flour, and powdered milk for the children. They brought all they could, but always there were more

Mayan men working in flower nursery near Indiantown.

people than food. Many Mexican Indians live in Chiapas, and I am sure they are as poor as any people in the world. But they, too, brought food to the Indian refugees from Guatemala, corn and beans, and I know many refugees would have starved without their help.

And there was always the awful waiting, for what we did not know. Rumors are terrible things in the refugee camps and settlements. We heard stories everyday that the Guatemalan army was massing on the border and that troops were going to enter the camps and force everyone to return to Guatemala. That never happened although sometimes small numbers of *kaibiles*—those are the special army forces that carried out most of the massacres in Guatemala—raided the camps and left quickly.

Rumors can be sad things, too. The longing to return to our homes was so great. One story swept through the camps like fire that a Guatemalan bishop was coming to the border with Red Cross workers to lead everyone safely home. My wife and children cried with joy when they heard the story. But it was not true. No one came.

In time, I found work picking tomatoes, and then things became a little better for us. At least we could now buy enough food and a few clothes, but there was no money for a better place to live. When the wet season came, rain poured through our *champa* day and night. All of our children became ill and had bad coughs. The church workers gave us some medicine, but our youngest son became worse and would not eat.

After eight months there was still not the slightest hope that we could return to our home in Huehuetenango. One morning I stood beside our *champa* watching my wife as she tried to cook some tortillas in the rain. Inside the *champa* my children were coughing. At that moment I made up my mind.

I said to my wife, "We cannot live under a tree any longer."

With the little money he had saved from picking tomatoes, Mr. Morales was able to buy food for his family as they made their way from the southern border to the northern border of Mexico. Finally, they crossed into Arizona and worked for several months as migrant workers. They moved slowly toward Indiantown where, Mr. Morales had heard, some Guatemalan Indians had found a place to live. The Morales family reached Indiantown in early 1983 and are living there today.

Mayan grandmother with grandchild, making tortillas, Indiantown.

≈ A SPECIAL PLACE

ONE OF THE first Mayan refugees to reach Indiantown came to the little Florida community because of its name. "I knew what Indian means in English," he says, "and I thought that Indiantown was a special place for Indians."

And so it proved to be. In this town that has seen and tried to cope with the misery of so many hard-luck migrants over the years, the outpouring of sympathy and help for the desperate Mayan Indians was immediate. Volunteers from the Holy Cross Catholic Church service center, always heavily overworked, found housing, clothes, and food for the new arrivals.

Citizens of Indiantown not connected with Holy Cross Church volunteered their time to help with health problems and with teaching the Maya the rudiments of surviving in their new home, including finding work in the fields and orchards. *The Country Scribe,* Indiantown's weekly newspaper, carried a fine series of articles about the Guatemalan Indians, the terror they had fled from, and the culture of their ancient Mayan ancestors.

Mayan families in Indiantown.

Mayan women receiving health instruction at Blue Camp, Indiantown. The teacher is a Kanjobal-speaking Guatemalan Indian, educated at San Carlos University, Guatemala City. He is seeking political asylum in the United States.

Claire Siefker is one of those who saw the need and responded to it. A resident of Indiantown for twenty-one years, Mrs. Siefker helps her husband in his construction business and has raised six children, but she always has made time to help in a community that never has all the help it needs. She studied for a year to become a technician in the town's medical emergency program, which included volunteer ambulance service.

"I know all the medical people in this town," Claire Siefker says.

That is one reason why, in 1983, she began teaching a health care class for adult Maya. Mrs. Siefker has visited Guatemala. She knows about the way Guatemalan women wash clothes at the public fountain or the river and how they keep their children and themselves clean in their sweat baths. But there are no *pilas* or *temascals* in Indiantown. Instead there are laundromats, showers, and bathtubs.

"We had to show them how to use these things," Mrs. Siefker says, "how to keep from scalding themselves and their children. And I mean *show*, not just tell. You try translating instructions from English to Spanish to Kanjobal about what shampoo is and how to use it or the steps you go through in using a washing machine and see how much gets through. You just keep doing it until they understand."

The Mayan men were getting jobs in the fields and orchards around Indiantown. Every evening they came home from working in an environment where contact with pesticides is a part of life. They knew nothing about pesticides, nothing about washing thoroughly with a disinfectant soap and about getting their clothes clean before wearing them again.

"There were some bad skin problems at first," Mrs. Siefker says, "but they learned."

The Mayan women learned about many things: how to cook tortillas on a gas stove, how to shop in a supermarket when the labels on the cans and packages are unintelligible, how to get help at the health clinic, how to take advantage of the abundant vegetables and fruits around Indiantown for a nutritious diet. The Guatemalans wanted to learn English, so Claire Siefker and half a dozen other Indiantown residents, including a retired tugboat captain, became English teachers in night classes. The Maya were shy and found the new language strange and difficult, but some of them have kept coming to class, even after a long day in the fields.

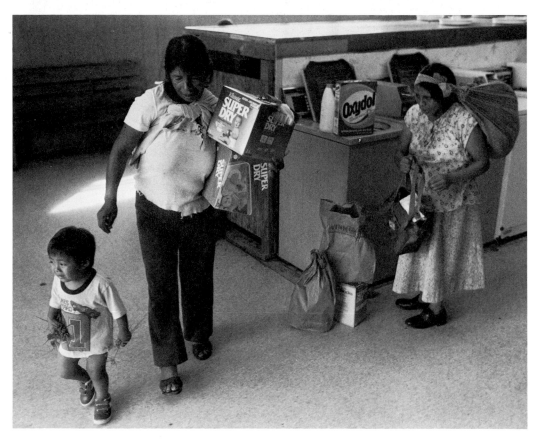

The laundromat has taken the place of the village pila for Guatemalan Mayan women in Indiantown.

Sister Carol Putnam helps a young Mayan man learn English. Before escaping from Guatemala, he was forced to watch the massacre of eighteen people in his village.

Three Mayan girls in Migrant Head Start Program for preschoolers.

The Mayan children have bloomed in Indiantown. The first ne-
cessity for them was to regain health, and that has happened with a
good diet, roofs over their heads that held out the rain, and medicine
when it was needed. Some of the preschoolers have been able to
attend the splendid Migrant Head Start Program in Indiantown because their parents qualify as migrant farmworkers. In that program
they not only get two good meals a day but also a kind of health and
educational attention that they have never had before.

Very few of the Mayan children had any formal schooling when they arrived in Florida; some had been born in refugee camps in Mexico and had never known any kind of normal life. "I had never had a pencil in my hand before I started school," says a Mayan girl in second grade in Indiantown. "I did not know how to hold it." Then she adds proudly, "But now I can write."

One of the first concerns of the Mayan parents was that their children have a chance to go to school. Hope Rural School provided that chance for many of them at the primary level. The kindergarten through fourth grade school on the compound of Holy Cross Church was started in 1980 by Sister Carol to meet the special needs of migrant children. They are "the leftovers, the secondhand kids," as Sister Carol calls them, whose schooling is often a jumble of moving from one place to another and learning very little in the process.

Hope Rural School concentrates on the fundamentals—reading, writing, arithmetic. That is the foundation the students must have when they move from school to school. School hours are longer than those of most schools because the parents don't return from the citrus groves and vegetable fields until late. All teachers at the school are aware of the children's special needs, particularly in English, since many of those enrolled come from Spanish-speaking parents.

About half of the children enrolled at Hope Rural School come from permanent Indiantown families, however. "We have no intention of isolating the migrant children," says Sister Carol.

Such a school with its special goals and focus proved to be exactly right for the Mayan children. Although they all have started from absolute zero, most have made good progress, and in 1986 the "graduating" class of those ready to move on to the public school fifth grade will have several Mayan children in it.

While bicycles, ice cream, and trips to the beach quickly have become a part of the Mayan children's lives, the scars of the past are

Mayan children are enjoying life in Indiantown.

This photograph shows the ethnic variety of students at Hope Rural School.

still close to the surface and may be for a very long time. Once when a helicopter landed on the Hope Rural School grounds, bringing a news team from a television station in Miami, most of the children ran outside to see the excitement. But the Mayan boys and girls hid under their desks and cowered in the classroom corners. To them a helicopter meant soldiers, bullets, and death.

One day in Indiantown, a Guatemalan boy was watching when a uniformed border patrol officer walked up to question the boy's father. The boy saw that the officer had a gun strapped to his hip, and he was terrified. He was sure that the officer was going to shoot his father.

"We had just arrived," the boy said later, "and I thought he was a soldier like the ones in Guatemala."

Now the boy and the other Mayan children in Indiantown have learned the difference.

⌇ AN UNCERTAIN FUTURE

THE THREAT of being sent back to Guatemala is the darkest cloud hovering over the Mayan Indians in Indiantown and for others who have sought refuge in Arizona and California. Just a few days after their arrival in Indiantown, six Guatemalans were picked up by the border patrol and taken to the Krome Detention Center for illegal aliens in Miami. They were separated from their children, who were cared for by other Mayan families.

Father Frank O'Loughlin, the parish priest at Holy Cross Catholic Church in Indiantown, spends a great deal of his time fighting for a better life for migrant farmworkers. He quickly took to heart the plight of the Mayan Indians and led the community efforts to help them. When word reached him that some of the Guatemalans had been taken to the detention center, he went immediately to Miami to get them out.

Few things are harder than battling the immigration bureaucracy, but Father Frank is a battler. He is also an Irish immigrant and naturalized U.S. citizen that one newspaper reporter admiringly de-

Father Frank O'Loughlin with Guatemalan children.

scribed as a street fighter. The priest sought the help of civil rights lawyers with the American Friends Service Committee and Florida Rural Legal Services. It took them almost two months, but they finally got a federal judge to release the Guatemalans. But the release was only temporary while they waited for the immigration court to rule on their applications for asylum as refugees.

The Maya in Indiantown have put their hopes of staying legally in the country entirely in the hands of the civil rights lawyers, who must present each case to the court individually. Immigration laws are meaningless to the Guatemalans, although they know only too well the dangers they face if they are returned to their country. Some have heard from relatives and friends in Guatemala that others who have returned to their homes have been killed.

"To go back is to die," said one of the Maya.

United States immigration law defines a refugee as a person who had fled from his country because of political or religious persecution. The Mayan Indians of Guatemala fit that definition to tragic perfection. The U.S. State Department, however, has taken the position that the Maya who have come to the United States are not refugees and that it is safe for them to return to Guatemala.

It is true that the level of violence in Guatemala is not as high as when the Maya fled from the country. But well-documented reports in 1985 by Amnesty International and the Washington Office on Latin America, a human rights organization that receives church support, make clear that the refugees would be in extreme danger if they returned. Reports published in 1985 in both *The New York Times* and *The Washington Post* describe continued violence in the Indian areas of Guatemala.

"It is our opinion that if they were returned, they would be in danger," says Peter Upton, an attorney with American Friends Service Committee in Miami.

Rob Williams of Florida Rural Legal Services points out that the State Department advises Americans visiting Guatemala not to go to Huehuetenango. "If it's not safe for Americans, what must it be like for these people?" he asks.

Further evidence that returning to Guatemala would be dangerous for the Maya who have fled is the fact that Mexico continues to give asylum to the tens of thousands who have sought refuge there. The Mexican government does this even though the presence of the

Maya is a financial burden and strains relations between their country and Guatemala.

Perhaps the most appropriate comment on the State Department's position came from a biting editorial in Indiantown's *Country Scribe* newspaper:

> We received an appeal in the mail this week for funds from Ellis Island Foundation, seeking a donation to help restore the famous island and the even more famous Statue of Liberty which rises above it. Of course we need to keep intact and in good condition the world's most inspiring symbol of freedom.
>
> But we also need to keep intact the day-to-day actions which demonstrate our willingness to back up our philosophy with deeds consistent with the symbol; that is why Indiantown's population of Mayan Indians seems so important to our view of freedom and liberty. . . .
>
> Anthropologists might suggest our duty to prevent the genocide of an ancient, indigenous people; we would rather suggest the irony of restoring the Statue of Liberty, while sending a peaceful people to their death by returning them to a homeland horror.

Fortunately for the Mayan Indians, the State Department cannot on its own authority send them back to Guatemala. The decision as to whether they receive refugee status or at least are allowed to stay in the United States until they can safely return to Guatemala is up to the courts. First, there is the immigration court and then, if necessary, the United States Court of Appeals. All of this takes time; and if all else fails, the civil rights lawyers intend to take their case directly to Congress.

A main concern of those helping the Guatemalans is what the

Neil Boothby with Mayan children.

effect of being uprooted again might have on the Mayan children. To help answer that question, Peter Upton asked Neil Boothby to come to Indiantown and get to know the Mayan children. To prepare his arguments for the courts, Upton needed to know as much as he could about how the Mayan children were still affected by what had happened to them in Guatemala and about how well they were adjusting in Indiantown. Upton needed the insights and judgments of an experienced psychologist.

That is what Neil Boothby is. Educated at Harvard as a clinical child psychologist, he has worked in both Asia and Africa helping refugee children who are victims of war and political violence. Boothby said yes to Upton and came to Indiantown with his wife and young son. It was not a short visit. They arrived in September, 1984, and stayed until July, 1985.

A Mayan boy's happier memory of his home in Guatemala. The bird is the quetzal, with a long beautiful green tail. The quetzal, Guatemala's national bird, symbolizes freedom.

Boothby selected a group of Mayan children between the ages of six and eighteen and learned everything he could about them. He talked to each one of them individually a number of times, watched them in the classrooms and on the playgrounds, visited them in their homes and got to know their parents. He talked to their teachers and others in Indiantown who knew them. When he was finished he knew their personal and family histories, and he knew them.

One way of finding out what was in the Mayan children's minds was to ask them to draw pictures about their past life in Guatemala.

Mayan child's drawing of his village in Guatemala being bombed by army planes. "They just do it," the boy said. "I don't know why."

Some of the pictures they drew were of mountains, birds, flowers, and village life that they remembered fondly from their lives there. But other pictures were very different. They were of planes dropping bombs on villages, helicopters pouring bullets down on people, soldiers attacking a village, guerrillas killing a man. In gently questioning the children, Boothby learned that these were scenes they had witnessed or been a part of, sometimes more than once. Talking about them was hard for some of the Mayan children, and there was no doubt that the memories were indelibly imprinted in their minds.

Mayan child's drawing of army helicopter firing bullets at people praying in front of church in her village. "I saw it all," she said.

One of the boys had seen soldiers decapitate a guerrilla. When he told the psychologist about it, he spoke in a whisper and his face was sweaty. "I saw it all," he said, "but they didn't see me."

While the Mayan children had some good memories of Guatemala, Boothby learned that fear and anxiety were the emotions closest to the surface when he asked them if they ever thought about returning to their country. From watching them play at school, Boothby discovered that, when angry at missing a turn on a swing or being left out of a game, the worst threat that one Mayan child could hurl at another was, "The teachers are going to send you back to Guatemala!"

Boothby puts it very clearly. "They are children who have been through too much violence, known too much fear. They have seen too much human suffering in Guatemala and Mexico."

His recommendation is equally clear: "If you want to do the best thing for the children, you will let them stay in Indiantown where they have adjusted well and made strong attachments in the school and community. You won't even let it get into their minds that they might be sent back to Guatemala."

To say that the Maya's adjustment to life in Indiantown has been easy would be to deny reality. Moving from one world into another can never be easy. But they have accepted the new life for themselves and their children and have made up their minds that it will be as good a life as possible. Yet they are Mayan Indians and have roots in a culture that is one of the most ancient on earth. Some of the memories, some of the links with the past, will fade, but some will remain.

They brought with them a sense of caring that shows no sign of disappearing in their strange new environment. When they must travel as migrant workers, some leave their children with friends who they know will treat them as their own. Several of the families have with them children left orphaned by the terror in Guatemala. All the Maya want to know what is going on in each other's lives, and they try to help when help is needed.

They brought with them a gentleness and a contemplative spirit that have not faded. Sister Carol says that in three years she has known of only two fights among the Mayan men, both caused by alcohol. Sister Esperanza describes the way the children love to look for wild flowers and to watch the many birds that inhabit this town on the edge of the Everglades.

Guatemalan refugees relaxing on a Sunday afternoon.

Once Sister Esperanza saw three little Mayan girls sitting quietly on a step at school. "What are you doing?" she asked.

"Watching the grass grow," one of them answered.

Already the Maya in Indiantown have begun to have a Fiesta of San Miguel in September just as it would be in Guatemala. They eat the special foods, fly kites, sing happy songs and sad songs. They have a mirimba, which is an ancient Mayan musical instrument, and it is made of hormiga wood from the Guatemalan forests, as all true mirimbas must be. The mirimba was brought piece by piece from Guatemala, and it is now kept in the church as a great treasure. At special times it is played all day and all night. Several of the Mayan

Communion at Holy Cross Church.

A Maya at prayer.

men know how to play it, both popular songs and the sacred music of the Maya that reaches far back into the past.

Holy Cross Church also provides a link with their past village life. Every Sunday a special mass is said in Spanish. The familiar songs are sung, and some words of Kanjobal are always a part of the service. Whole families attend, husbands, wives, children, grandparents. A bus brings those who are living in migrant camps outside of town, and Sunday mass provides an opportunity to find out what is happening in the lives of others and to exchange any news that might have come from Huehuetenango. Such news belongs to every Maya and is important in their lives.

In one corner of the chapel are pictures of priests and nuns who have been killed in the violence in Central America. The pictures of twenty-one martyred priests from Guatemala outnumber all the others combined. The Maya look at the pictures, but they need no reminder of the fury in their country from which they sought and found refuge in this small town in Florida.

Additional Facts About Guatemala

Size: 42,042 square miles (approximately the size of the state of Tennessee). Guatemala is the third largest Central American country: smaller than Honduras and Nicaragua, larger than El Salvador, Panama, and Belize.

Population: Guatemala's 7.5 million people make it the most populous Central American nation. About 50 percent are native Guatemalan Indians. The other 50 percent are of mixed Spanish-Indian descent called *ladinos.*

Language: Spanish is the official language, but the Indians of Guatemala speak twenty-two different languages and over one hundred dialects.

Religion: Eighty percent Catholic, 20 percent Protestant. Most Guatemalan Indians, although embracing Christianity, are also guided by the religious beliefs of their ancient Mayan ancestors.

Health: Life expectancy is 56 years for urban Guatemalans, 41 years in rural areas. (Average life expectancy in the United States is 73 years.)

Literacy: Only 45 percent of the adult population can read (compared to 77.4 percent in the rest of Central America).

Economy: Guatemala has the strongest economy in the region, with a gross national product of $7.5 billion in 1980. Its major exports are coffee, cotton, sugar, bananas, and beef. Almost two hundred United States corporations have invested $300 million in Guatemala.

Land Distribution: Two percent of the population own 70 percent of the land. Almost all high quality land is owned by a few thousand persons.

Income Distribution: Five percent of the population receive 59 percent of the national income. The poorest 50 percent receive 7 percent. Seventy-five percent of the population have a per capita income of less than $300 per year.

Government: Officially Guatemala is a democracy with a president elected every four years. In fact, the country has been ruled for the past thirty years by military dictators. The present military ruler is General Mejia Victores, who assumed power in a military coup in August, 1983. However, the present military dictator, General Mejia Victores, is scheduled to step down in January, 1986, in favor of a popularly elected president.

The United States and Guatemala

FOR THE United States, Guatemala is ultimately the most important Central American country. It has the strongest economy and the largest population. Its oil reserves are estimated at 5 billion barrels. It shares a long and easy-to-cross border with Mexico, which shares the same kind of border with the United States.

Guatemala presents the United States with one of its most difficult problems in foreign policy. Deeply concerned about the spread of communism in Central America, the United States government does not want to do anything to encourage political instability in Guatemala. But the alternative of supporting brutal military dictators has troubled Congress and some administrations for a number of years.

Congress has tried to solve this unhappy dilemma, at least in part, by prohibiting the sending of military equipment to Guatemala. Congress has also specified that all economic aid be directed to programs intended to help the poorer classes. The present administration wants to resume sending military equipment to Guatemala, but Congress has indicated that it will continue to say no until the Guatemalan government can demonstrate that it has stopped unnecessary violence against its people.

The problems of the United States in its relations with Guatemala (and with its other Central American neighbors) raise many questions to which no easy answers will be found. But Congress surely is on the right track in tying military aid to an improvement in Guatemala's human rights record and in trying to ensure that economic aid will help the poor and not simply make the wealthy minority in Guatemala richer still.

In December, 1985, Guatemalan voters chose a civilian president, Marco Vinicio Cerezo Arevalo, in an orderly, violence-free election. He will assume office in January, 1986. This is a highly encouraging development, but even optimistic political observers caution that a true growth of the democratic process will not come easily in this Central American country so long ruled by military dictators.

Bibliography

Books

Bleeker, Sonia. *The Maya: Indians of Central America.* New York: William Morrow & Co., Inc., 1961.

Cheney, Glenn Alan. *El Salvador: Country in Crisis.* New York: Franklin Watts, Inc., 1982.

_____. *Revolution in Central America.* New York: Franklin Watts, Inc., 1984.

Karen, Ruth. *Song of the Quail: The Wondrous World of the Maya.* New York: Four Winds Press, 1972.

La Farge, Oliver and Douglas Byers. *The Year Bearer's People.* Department of Middle American Research, Tulane University, 1931.

Oakes, Maud. *Beyond the Windy Place.* New York: Farrar, Straus, 1951.

_____. *The Two Crosses of Todos Santos: Survivals of Mayan Religious Ritual.* New York: Pantheon Books, Inc., 1951.

Schlesinger, Stephen and Stephen Kinzer. *Bitter Fruit: The Untold Story of the American Coup in Guatemala.* New York: Doubleday & Co., Inc., 1982.

Sexton, James D. *Campesino: The Diary of a Guatemalan Indian.* Tucson: The University of Arizona Press, 1985.

Special Reports and Articles

"Bitter and Cruel. . .": Report of a Mission to Guatemala by the British Parliamentary Human Rights Group, October, 1984. London, 1985.

"Disappearances" in Guatemala Under the Government of General Oscar Humberto Mejia Victores (August, 1983—January, 1985). Amnesty International, March, 1985.

Guatemala: A Government Program of Political Murder. Amnesty International. London, February, 1981.

Guatemala: Government Against the People: Witnesses of Indian Massacres, March-September 1982. Prepared for the Conference on Human Rights in Guatemala, organized by Johns Hopkins School for Advanced International Studies and the Washington Office on Latin America, Washington, D. C., October 21, 1982.

Human Rights in Guatemala. United States Congress: Hearings before the Subcommittes on Human Rights and International Organizations and on Inter-American Affairs of the Committee on Foreign Affairs, House of Representatives, 94th Congress, July 30, 1981.

Human Rights in Nicaragua, Guatemala, and El Salvador: Implications for U. S. Policy. Hearing before the Subcommittee on International Organizations, Committee on International Relations, House of Representatives, June 8 and 9, 1976.

Little Hope: Human Rights in Guatemala, January 1984 to January 1985. Americas Watch. New York, February, 1985.

"New Army Slayings in Guatemala Reported by Villagers and Church" by James LeMoyne, *The New York Times,* July 28, 1985.

Report on the Situation of Human Rights in the Republic of Guatemala. Organization of American States, Washington, D.C., October, 1981.

"Strangers in a Strange Land" by Angie Cannon. *Tropic* magazine, *The Miami Herald,* May 5, 1985.

"Troubled Guatemala Moves Toward Vote" by Robert J. McCartney. *The Washington Post,* July 24, 1985.

Without Security or Development: Guatemala Militarized by Chris Krueger and Kjell Enge. Washington Office on Latin America. Washington, D.C., June 6, 1985.

Witness to Genocide: The Present Situation of Indians in Guatemala by Craig W. Nelson and Kenneth I. Taylor, Legal Commentary by Janice Kruger. Survival International, London, 1983.

Witnesses to Political Violence in Guatemala by Shelton H. Davis and Julie Hodson. Oxfam America, 1982.

INDEX